# CLICK!

# CLICK!

## *A Story about George Eastman*

by Barbara Mitchell
illustrations by Jan Hosking Smith

A Carolrhoda Creative Minds Book

Carolrhoda Books, Inc./Minneapolis

*For Keith Leaman and his cameras*

Text copyright © 1986 by Barbara Mitchell
Illustrations copyright © 1986 by Carolrhoda Books, Inc.
All rights reserved. International copyright secured. No part of this book
may be reproduced in any form whatsoever without permission in writing
from the publisher except for the inclusion of brief quotations in an
acknowledged review.
Manufactured in the United States of America

*This book is available in two editions:*
Library binding by Carolrhoda Books, Inc.
Soft cover by First Avenue Editions
241 First Avenue North
Minneapolis, Minnesota 55401

LIBRARY OF CONGRESS CATALOGING-IN-PUBLICATION DATA

Mitchell, Barbara, 1941-
  CLICK! A story about George Eastman.

  (A Carolrhoda creative minds book)
  Summary: Follows the life and career of the man
who revolutionized photography by developing a camera
simple enough for anyone to use.
  1. Eastman, George, 1854-1932—Juvenile literature.
2. Photographic industry—United States—Biography—
Juvenile literature. [1. Eastman, George, 1854-1932.
2. Inventors. 3. Photography—History]
I. Hosking Smith, Jan, ill. II. Title. III. Series.
TR140.E3M58   1986      338.7′6177[B][92]      86-2672
ISBN 0-87614-289-7 (lib. bdg.)
ISBN 0-87614-472-5 (pbk.)

  3   4   5   6   7   8   9   10   96   95   94   93   92   91   90   89   88

# Table of Contents

# Chapter One

George had a toothache. He did not want to trouble his mother about it, though. The Eastmans had hardly enough money to keep the house going, let alone enough to pay a dentist.

Mrs. Eastman was already bustling about in the kitchen getting breakfast for George, Ellen Maria, and Emma Kate—and for the boarders. The boarders had come after Father died. "*Boarders on Livingston Park,*" the neighbors had said. They did not think much of having the homes in this stylish neighborhood of Rochester, New York, turned into rooming houses. But Mr. Eastman had sunk all of his money into his dream, a business college for the city of Rochester, and very little was left when he died.

George watched his mother ladle out big bowls of oatmeal. She looked tired. Probably has one of her headaches again, he thought. After breakfast would come the great stack of dishes to wash, the rooms to clean, and the laundry to do. Then there would be Katey's lessons to hear. Emma Kate had been crippled by polio and could not get to school during the winter.

George did not like to see his pretty mother struggling so. It worried him. It frightened him, too. The house was chilly again this morning. The wood pile would have to last all winter, Mother had said. But suppose the wood pile did *not* last? What would they do? "Maybe I could get a job, Mother," George said.

Mrs. Eastman looked up from her serving. More than anything, she wanted her children to finish school. "Nine-year-old boys are too young to be thinking about jobs," she said to George. "Now run along to Sunday school."

George took his place in the row of Sunday school boys. He had brought along something interesting, just in case the lesson went on too long. It was a puzzle he had made out of his mother's old wire knitting needles. The wonderful toy went up and down the row of curious boys.

The boy next to George wanted George to give the toy to him for keeps. "Nothing doing," George said. Then George had an idea. "All right, you may have it—for 10¢," he said. George took the dime home to his mother.

By the time George was 13, the Eastmans were nearly penniless. An insurance agent offered George a job as a messenger boy. There was nothing for Mrs. Eastman to do but give in and let her son leave school to go to work. George made $3 a week and started his first cash-and-account book. Like everything else of George's, the book was a masterpiece of organization. He even wrote in the money he spent to treat his family to ice cream on his fourteenth birthday: "ice cream, 65¢, July 12, 1868."

The next year, George got a job as an office boy. "You certainly are an organizer," his boss said. Soon George was earning $35 a month. He liked to do things for his mother whenever he could. Once he took her to a lecture and afterward had a photograph taken of himself for her (and one taken for his Sunday school teacher, too).

Having a photograph taken was a real labor of love (both for the photographer and for the subject). One had to sit absolutely still while the photographer darted in and out of his black hood and fussed about with his glass plates, getting everything just so. But when it was all over, one went out with a magical likeness of oneself. Portrait parlors were all the rage, and nobody was more fascinated by them than George Eastman.

When George's fifteenth birthday came, his Uncle Horace sent him $10. George bought a jackknife and some photographs and frames for himself, and a century plant for his mother. The popular ornamental plant would cheer her up, George thought. Mrs. Eastman loved flowers and plants. It would be fun for the girls as well. The plant had come all the way from Mexico and, according to tradition, was not supposed to bloom until it was a century old.

"Someday I shall fill your house with flowers," George said when he presented his mother with the surprise gift.

"That would be very nice, George," Mrs. Eastman said. She wondered if her son had any idea what it would cost to fill a house with flowers.

## Chapter Two

In 1874, George got a job as a junior book-keeper at the Rochester Savings Bank. George was 20 now, and he considered himself truly the man of the family. Not only was he able to keep the bills paid, but there was a little money to put into the bank as well.

"I need a hobby," George said one day, "something to relax with when I get home from the bank each day." So he bought himself a flute on the installment plan. "Someday I shall fill your house with music, Mother," he said.

"That would be very nice, George," replied Mrs. Eastman.

Unfortunately, George's progress on the flute went even slower than the payments. He hurried home from the bank each afternoon to practice "Annie Laurie." After two years, George's version of "Annie Laurie" still sounded nothing at all like the popular version of the song. "Maybe the flute is not my hobby," George said. So he took up horseback riding instead. "I feel much better getting out into the fresh air each day," he said. But he wasn't overly in love with horses.

When he had been at the bank for several years, George decided it was time he had a vacation. "You deserve it, George," his banker friends said. "Where will you go? To the beach? A few days in the mountains, maybe?"

"I think I shall go to Santo Domingo," George said quietly.

His friends sat up straight in their chairs. "Santo Domingo! George! It is not every day that one goes to Central America. You should buy a camera and take pictures of your trip." (One of the other bank workers had recently been in Santo Domingo and had returned with stunning photographs.)

George discovered that buying a camera was a big project. In the 1870s, there was no such thing as a candy bar-sized camera to tuck into one's pocket. George soon found that he needed close to 50 pounds of equipment. A Rochester photographer happily supplied him with a basic outfit. "It has a camera the size of a soapbox," George reported to his bank friends. Then there was the tripod to hold it, "strong and heavy enough to support a bungalow," George said. There was the dark tent, big enough for George to crawl into.

There was no such thing as film in the 1870s. Photographers took pictures with glass plates. The plates were coated with a chemical mixture called collodion. Then they were made sensitive to light by being bathed in silver nitrate. While it was still wet, the plate was exposed in the camera. The picture had to be developed then and there, before the plate dried. So outdoor photographers carried their darkrooms with them.

George paid $5 for lessons, "to learn what to do with all the stuff," he explained. And with all of this, there were numerous smaller necessities to purchase. George became so involved with all of his new equipment that he forgot all about going to Santo Domingo. It didn't matter, though. The idea of the trip had opened up the world of photography to him.

The day finally came when George was ready

to go out into the country to take some pictures. He spread his equipment about him and numbered it all. (It was easier to keep track of that way.)

1. plate holder
2. box of glass plates
3. trays
4. bottles of chemicals
5. stirring rods
6. measuring glasses
7. jug for water
8. dark tent
9. tripod
10. camera

Mrs. Eastman stood watching. "How long will you be gone, George?" she asked.

"Oh, just for the afternoon." He loaded the whole pile onto his back and set off for the outskirts of Rochester.

Mrs. Eastman looked on anxiously as her son made his way down the street. Perhaps he should have bought a wheelbarrow as well, she thought.

George clumped along, not very quickly, but happily. He was an "in-the-field" photographer.

As soon as he hit the open country, some farmers' children began to tag after him. "It's an organ grinder!" they cried. "Play us some music!"

George barely noticed the clamoring children. His eyes were fixed on the picturesque view ahead. Ah, a picture, he thought. He set up his dark tent and then the tripod. He placed his soapbox-sized camera on its sturdy holder and pointed it at the beautiful New York countryside. He crawled back into his dark tent and spread collodion on a glass plate. He dipped the plate into its nitrate bath. The plate clouded over beautifully. It was time to take the picture.

With the plate still dripping in its holder, George rushed back to his camera. He snapped the picture and then rushed the plate back into the dark tent to develop the shot.

Developing was tricky. George concentrated with all his might inside the smelly, stuffy black tent. He completely forgot the sunny world outside. Developing a picture took anywhere from 40 minutes to an hour. CLIP-CLOP-CLIP-CLOP. A farmer with his horse and wagon rumbled by. The sudden noise startled George. SMASH. There went the glass plate. Drat! George took a fresh plate and began the whole process all over again.

When the sun began to set, George packed up his miniature chemical laboratory and headed for home. His face was streaked with sweat. His pants were covered with dust. His hands and shirt were stained with chemicals. In his pocket were three photographs. "Well, what do you think of photography in the field?" his banker friends asked on Monday morning.

"I love it," George said.

George had at last found his hobby. Anytime the bank was closed, he was out taking pictures. If he wasn't taking them, he was reading about taking them. He began to study French. The French were fine photographers, and George didn't want to miss anything they had to say about his new hobby.

Instead of going to Santo Domingo, George went to Michigan's Mackinac Island to photograph the natural bridge there. Packing for a photographer's vacation was an awesome task. In addition to all his photographic apparatus, George had a trunk full of clothes to lug. The biggest problem, though, was what to do with the silver nitrate. Silver nitrate was an acid. It had to be carried in a leak-proof glass container. If it spilled, it would burn holes in whatever it touched. George wrapped the little glass bottle of nitrate in his underwear and tucked it gently into his trunk.

George arrived on Mackinac Island to find that the bottle had leaked in spite of his careful efforts. He began his photographer's vacation with a trip to the store to buy new underwear.

The day he set out to take the bridge picture was broiling hot. George set up his equipment and disappeared into his black tent. Meanwhile, a group of tourists strolled by. "A photographer!" they cried. They draped themselves over the bridge in picturesque poses. When George came out to take his picture, he was so intent on focusing his camera on the scenery that he hardly noticed the tourists. After taking the picture, he disappeared into his tent again.

The tourists waited eagerly for him to reappear. The minutes ticked by. The sun got hotter and hotter. "What in the world is he doing in there?" a perspiring tourist asked.

George crawled out of his steamy tent at last. The tourists came running. "How much is the photo?" they asked.

George was stunned. "Why, it is not for sale," he said. "I am not a professional photographer.

I'm just an amateur out enjoying my hobby."

The tourists were not pleased. "Then why did you keep us standing here for nearly an hour in the broiling sun while you fooled around in your tent?" one of them demanded.

"You ought to wear a sign saying *amateur*," another disgruntled model said. The disappointed group went off in a huff.

A crowd gathered everywhere George went. But it didn't bother him. What did bother him was the amount of equipment he had to tote. "There ought to be a way to take pictures without carting around such a packhorse of a load," he said. George began to dream of a way.

# Chapter Three

The whole problem is this *wet* plate business, George decided. In a photography magazine from England, he read that photographers there were now using *dry* plates. The English plates were covered with a gelatine emulsion—a jelled mixture of chemicals that remained sensitive to light even after it had dried. English photographers were making their plates ready at home, tripping lightly off to the field, and doing their developing back at home. Oh, the wonder of it! No more toting big black tents around. No more runny collodion and nitrate solutions. (No more holey underwear!) George began to put all of his spare time into working out his own gelatine emulsion formula.

The Eastman kitchen reeked of chemicals every night. Mrs. Eastman poked her head in every hour or so. "George, will you please go to bed! You have to be at the bank in the morning."

George glanced up from his stoveful of bubbling pots. "Yes, Mother."

He went right on with his mixing and cooking. Some nights he got so tired that he fell asleep right on the kitchen floor. Mrs. Eastman fixed him a blanket and pillow by the stove. Still, there were nights when George simply worked on until morning. "George, you are getting as thin as pie crust," his mother scolded.

"I can sleep on the weekends," George said. And that is what he did, until, at last, he had a dry plate that satisfied him.

At first George had wanted to make dry plates just for his own convenience, but now he had another idea. "I cannot be the only photographer in America who is tired of lugging leaky collodion and nitrate bottles," he reasoned. He devised a machine that could turn out large numbers of his new dry plate and rented the third floor of a building in the middle of Rochester.

Just before Thanksgiving in 1880, George made an announcement. "Mother," he said, "I am going to be leaving the bank soon."

Mrs. Eastman looked up from her Thanksgiving preparations. "Leaving the bank, George?"

"Yes," said George, "I have it all well organized. I am going into the dry-plate business."

At that time, the Eastmans had a boarder named Colonel Henry A. Strong. The Colonel was a businessman himself. He admired 26-year-old George's confidence. "I'll put up $1,000 to get you started," he told George.

George left the bank. Now he could devote all of his time to photography. The Eastman Dry Plate Company opened officially on January 1, 1881. By November of that year, the company was turning out 4,000 plates a month. Orders poured in from happy photographers.

Not long afterward, though, the photographers were not so pleased. "Those new Eastman dry plates are going dead before we can use them," they complained. Orders stopped coming in.

George recalled all the plates for testing. Sure enough, every one came up red and foggy, just as the buyers had said. For the first time in his life, George Eastman was in debt. He slept in a hammock at the factory and threw himself into testing emulsions day and night.

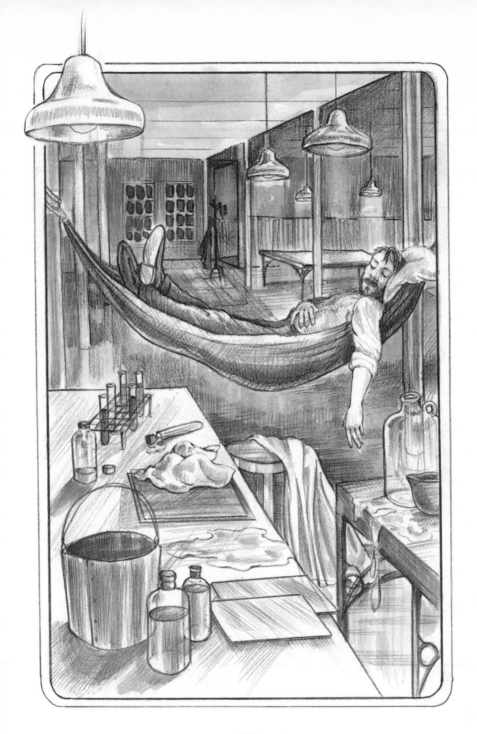

Mrs. Eastman worried about her son more than ever. "You must at least come home once in a while for a good square meal," she insisted. She went to the factory and hauled George home herself. "And George," she said, "you *must* do something to relax." So George bought himself a good supply of cowboy and detective books and read them while his emulsions cooked.

After 469 experiments, the results were still coming up the same—red fog. He could not expect his customers to take pictures with foggy plates. Still, he did not have the slightest idea what was causing the problem. He and Colonel Strong made a frantic trip to England. The English platemakers threw up their hands; they could not find anything wrong with George's formula either.

George and the Colonel came home more confused than ever. It was back to the bubbling pots again. Then, after 16 more experiments, the plates miraculously came up clear.

"What did you do, George?" the Colonel asked.

"Used a new supply of gelatine," George said.

All along the trouble had been with the supply of gelatine sent by the manufacturer. "You can bet the Eastman Dry Plate Company will test all materials from now on," George said joyfully as he settled down for a good night's sleep.

He didn't rest for long, though. "Wouldn't it be wonderful if photographers didn't have to use plates at all!" he thought. Now George's ambition was to make photography so simple that *anyone* could enjoy it. He began to experiment again.

The result of this new experiment was a strip of paper coated with collodion and a sensitized gelatine emulsion. George called his thin new product *film*. It was the first film in photographic history. By March 1885, the new paper-based film was ready for shipment. All the photographer had to do was wind the paper strip around a lightweight mahogony mechanism that could be fitted onto any camera. A clock key was used to wind the film. George saw great possibilities for sales. The previous fall, he had begun drawing up plans for a new and larger factory. Maybe now he could actually build it. "Everyone is sure to go to film," George said. Imagine, no more smashed plates when farmers' horses and wagons rumbled by! No more sitting ramrod still in portrait parlors while photographers fussed about with glass plates.

But the portrait-parlor photographers were not pleased at all with this invention.

"We have *always* used glass plates," they said. They rather enjoyed whipping their mysterious plates in and out of the camera while their subject sat mesmerized before them. Only a few of them tried George's film.

"In-the-field photographers are *sure* to go to film," George said—and they did. The problem was that there just were not many in-the-field photographers. Outdoor photography was an expensive hobby, and it was just too complicated for all but the most dedicated hobbyists. "I've got to come up with a simpler way to take pictures," George said.

# Chapter Four

George worked away quietly for three years. In the spring of 1888, he revealed his new camera. It was a wonder! The little box-shaped picture taker was meant to be held in the hands rather than set on a tripod. It weighed a mere 22 ounces and was just 6¾ inches deep and 3¾ inches wide. *Anyone* could use it. The owner did not even have to put in the film; the camera came already loaded. All one had to do was press a button. CLICK! The picture was taken.

Then the camera, precious pictures inside, was mailed back to the Eastman company. For $10, the manufacturer would develop and print the pictures, then return them with the camera—re-loaded of course—for more picture-taking fun.

There was no longer a need for a packhorse of a load, not even a need for a tripod. With all of this, the new little camera was inexpensive. For $25, the buyer got a camera, film, a carrying strap, and a leather case. All the new camera lacked was a name.

George solved that problem in short order. One night he sat down with paper and pen and began to doodle. What he wanted was a completely new word, something short and snappy. Something buyers could not help but remember. He wrote down the letter *K*. It was strong and had always been a favorite of his. In fact, why not put a *K* at the other end of the word as well, he thought. The letter *O* popped into his mind. *KO*. One by one, he tried other letters. *KOP*. "No personality," George said. He tried *KOU*. "Too easy to misspell." *KOD*. *KODAK*. It sounded just like the click the shutter made when the button was pushed on the new camera. That was it! The newest innovation in photography had a name.

Now it was up to George to convince the American public it *needed* a Kodak. He took out ads in every one of America's finest magazines. His ad was short and snappy: "Kodak cameras. You press the button—we do the rest."

film

1ST KODAK CAMERA

People who saw the ads were fascinated. "Does this mean that we can take pictures without having to know a thing about chemicals and printing?" they asked incredulously. They were soon rushing out to buy this new toy.

CLICK! CLICK-CLICK CLICK!

Taking "snapshots" became America's new pastime. George Eastman's little camera was revolutionizing the world of photography.

Once again George was working day and night, hardly able to keep up with the orders. He hired a secretary and a young chemist named Henry Reichenbach. George had been working to develop a strong, flexible film. (The paper-backed film tore easily and the grain of the paper was apt to show up in the finished picture.) He turned this research over to Reichenbach, and Reichenbach developed a transparent, flexible film made with celluloid. The orders came in faster than ever.

George came home one day in 1889 with startling news. "Mother," he said, "Our company is worth a million dollars."

"That is very nice, George," she said. By this time she was so used to her son doing what he set out to do that his announcement did not seem out of the ordinary to her.

The little third-floor factory was bursting at the seams with piled-up orders. One fine day that fall, George took a ride to the outskirts of Rochester and bought three farm properties. The plans for his new factory were about to become a reality. Before long, three modern buildings with the best machinery were going up—the beginnings of Kodak Park. In December 1889, the Eastman Kodak Company was incorporated.

Near the end of that summer, an order came in from Menlo Park, New Jersey, for one of the new little cameras. It was from Thomas Edison, the "electrical wizard." Edison used George's camera and film in the development of his motion-picture camera.

In 1891, the Eastman Kodak Company introduced another marvel—spooled film. The older film had to be wound outside the camera, which could only be done in a darkened room. The new spooled film was prewound, and photographers could load it into their cameras themselves in broad daylight. It would no longer be necessary to mail the whole camera back to Eastman Kodak.

By 1896, Eastman Kodak Company was turning out film and photographic paper by the mile every month. George went to London and Paris to establish plants. (He took his camera, of course. George still took pictures everywhere he went.) He came home to more startling news. The Kodak Park plant had just turned out its one hundred-thousandth camera.

Mass production made it possible for George to sell his cameras for less and less money. For the first time in history, just about any American with an average job could afford a camera. The new Bulls Eye sold for a mere $12. "It's the finest thing we've ever put out," George said proudly. "Practically foolproof." George thought a camera that did not work every time was worth nothing at all. Also introduced in 1896 was the Falcon, with a selling price of just $5.

George was to make one camera even less expensive; a camera that photographers still look back on with fondness. The only segment of the American public that perhaps could still not afford to buy a camera was the children, George realized. He remembered how he had loved photographs as a boy. Wouldn't it be fine, he thought, if boys and girls could take their own pictures. In 1900, he introduced the Brownie, intended especially for children. Its cost was only $1. George took out ads in children's magazines this time. Children were soon saving up their allowances for Brownies. Grandparents bought them as gifts—and one for themselves as well. It seemed that no one could resist the ingenious little gremlin of photography. "It works better than all the rest!" the picture-snapping grandparents exclaimed.

# Chapter Five

Gradually, George Eastman, who had once worried about the wood pile lasting through the winter, came to the realization that he was a millionaire. He quietly set about sharing his wealth. One of his first projects was a dental clinic for the city of Rochester. George had not forgotten what it was like to have a toothache and no money for the dentist. "I want the clinic accessible by all the streetcar lines," he insisted. Rochester children were soon hopping trolleys after school to have their teeth checked and cleaned for just 5¢. George later set up similar clinics in London, Paris, Rome, Stockholm, and Brussels—all of which were now home to an Eastman Kodak plant.

Nobody in Rochester should have to be without medical care, either, George believed. He sent for Colonel Henry A. Strong's daughter. (The businessman who had underwritten George's first business venture had since died.) "I feel that we should do something in honor of your father," he said. So along with another wealthy New York family, the Rockefellers, he set up the funds for the Henry A. Strong Memorial Hospital.

Many of George's chemists had come from the Massachusetts Institute of Technology. George wanted to make a gift to the school, so he wrote out a generous check and sent it as a donation from "Mr. Smith." (George did not like attention drawn to his giving.)

Not long afterward, a representative from the school came to him asking for a donation. George never let on that he had already made a contribution. He simply wrote out another check.

Another school to receive a gift from George Eastman was Tuskegee Institute in Alabama. Tuskegee, a school for black students, was struggling to survive; many of the students could not afford to pay the tuition that helped to keep the school going. A gifted botanist named George Washington Carver was doing great things there,

George thought. Also, he admired the dream that Booker T. Washington, the school's founder, had. At Tuskegee, students were taught academic and practical material to help them build a future, but most importantly they were taught to believe in themselves. George thought America ought to be paying more attention to the education of its black citizens.

George did not forget that long ago day when he had treated his mother to a lecture ticket, either. Working people ought to be able to go to concerts and lectures during their leisure hours, he believed. He established the Rochester Symphony and the Eastman School of Music. The music school was dear to his heart (despite his experience with "Annie Laurie"). George hung over the architects step by step. "The music hall must not be barny," he insisted. "I want it warm and rich in color."

When the beautiful concert hall was completed, the architects suggested to George that he have his portrait painted by a leading artist. "We want to hang it in a place of honor so that everyone who comes to the performances will see it," they said. The idea did not appeal at all to modest George Eastman. "I have an even better idea.

Why don't you have a giant sculpture made of me," he said, "with a camera in one hand and a horn in the other? You could place it up on the rooftop towering over your other figurines." No more was said of the portrait.

George could now afford to fill his mother's house with flowers and music, just as he had promised those many years ago. He built a 37-room mansion at 900 East Avenue in Rochester. The home reflected the Eastmans' quiet taste. George, as usual, supervised every detail. He filled the gardens with the old-fashioned flowers that were his mother's favorites. The greenhouse was filled with orchids and other exotic blooms. The rooms of the mansion were always fragrant with fresh-cut bouquets. Mrs. Eastman was to enjoy her mansion for only a few years, though. She died in 1918.

When the mansion was completed, George felt obliged to give a party. He held a New Year's Eve ball for 1,200 guests. A caterer provided the elegant food. Waiters wandered among the party goers with silver trays of hors d'oeuvres and champagne. In the midst of it all, George had a terrible realization. He did not know how to dance. While other young men had been attending

dancing classes and debutante balls, he had been working to build his business.

The Eastmans never gave a grand party again. They invited small groups of friends to Sunday night suppers instead. The guests would enjoy a light supper and then be entertained by a string quartet from the music school. "What would you like to serve this week, Mr. Eastman?" George's cook would ask. "Hash and beer. Or maybe baked beans," George was apt to reply. He wanted his guests to feel right at home.

The pipe organ at 900 East Avenue was one of George's great joys. He had his own personal organist, who arrived first thing in the morning. At 7:30 sharp, Mr. Gleason would begin to play, and George would come down the stairs accompanied by the glorious sounds of the great instrument. "Play anything but Bach," George always said. (George did not care for Bach.)

When George was about 50, he decided to take up camping. High in the mountains, deep in the forest, George could be just plain George Eastman. There was no need to live up to what people seemed to expect of a "rich man," and the cares of big business faded away. "We always had a bully time," George said.

But for George, camping out was no less complicated than city life. George camped in style. First there were the tents—the shower-bath tents, the cooking tents, and, of course, the sleeping tents. Then there was the smokehouse to take. George had made it himself for smoking the fish he loved to catch. There were his "camping clothes" to get ready. There were the pack animals to outfit. (George once took a train of 32 pack animals.) Of course there was the camera to take. It was fortunate for George that picture-taking equipment had been reduced to a compact camera that could easily be slipped into his trunk. He had a grand time just organizing all this before the camp-out even began.

George did the cooking himself on these outings. Late in the afternoon, he would disappear into the cooking tents. His guests waited for him to emerge as anxiously as those perspiring tourists had waited on Mackinac Island. Hash and beans might be good enough for Rochester Sunday night suppers, but George's camping guests feasted. George was likely to serve up roast elk or mountain grouse with wild rice. The grand finale was always one of George's homemade desserts. Out would come a fresh blueberry cobbler, or perhaps a lemon pie piled high with meringue. The guests always hoped for the most spectacular dessert of all: a tall, three-layer cake made with the cake mix George had invented for his camping trips. "That little Kodak you invented is fine, George," they would tease. "But we'll take your cake mix any time."

When George was 72, he decided to go on an African safari. (It turned out to be the first of a number of trips to Africa.) Now, *there* was something to organize. Tucked in with all the other necessary paraphernalia was always one of Mr. Edison's new home movie cameras. The highlight of one safari came when George had a chance to film a rhino. It was the biggest rhino George had ever seen. He took up Mr. Edison's camera and let the film roll.

There was barely a sound in the stillness of the African morning, just the click-click-click of George's film going around and around—and the CLUMP-CLUMP of the rhino. The rhino—not knowing that its picture was being taken—went right on with its morning walk. Closer and closer it came to film-rolling George.

Suddenly the huge beast charged. The hunter with George's party quickly took up his gun.

The African guide stood awestruck. Did this American visitor not know the danger of a charging rhino? George stood calmly, filming away.

Now he and the rhino were face-to-face. When the beast was a mere 15 paces from George, the hunter fired. George stopped the film, just before the rhino fell. His helpers came running. "Mr. Eastman! You might have been killed!"

George put down his camera. "Well, you have to trust in your organization," he said quietly.